The Wizard's Hat

Barbara Mitchelhill

Illustrated by Lisa Smith

OXFORD
UNIVERSITY PRESS

The wizard was cross.
"I've lost my magic hat," he said.

He looked and looked but he did
not see it.
"No hat! No magic!" he said.

His cat jumped down.
"I can see your hat," she said.
"Come with me."

The cat ran off but the wizard did not see where she went.

"Come back!" shouted the wizard.
But the cat did not come.

Now the wizard was very cross.
"I've lost my cat **and** my hat," said
the wizard.
"No cat! No hat! No magic!"

A bat went to help the wizard.
"I can see your hat," she said.
"Come with me."

The bat flew off but the wizard did
not see where she went.

"Come back!" shouted the wizard.
But the bat did not come.

Now the wizard was very, very cross.
"I've lost my cat **and** my bat **and**
my hat," he said.
"No cat! No bat! No hat! No magic!"

"I can help you," said a spider.
"How can you help me?" said the
wizard.

"Put on your glasses," said the spider.
The wizard put on his glasses.

"I can see the cat," said the wizard,
"and I can see the bat."

"And there is your hat,"
said the cat and the bat.
"It was there all the time."

"That **is** magic," said the wizard.

220